AF081646

**WITHDRAWN**
by
JEFFERSON COUNTY
PUBLIC LIBRARY, CO

# COUNTING BREATHS with the Count

### A Book about Mindfulness

Katherine Lewis

Lerner Publications ◆ Minneapolis

Sesame Street's mission has always been about teaching kids much more than simply the ABCs and 123s. This series of books about nurturing the positive character traits of mindfulness, gratitude, self-confidence, and responsibility will help children grow into the best versions of themselves. So come along with your funny, furry friends from Sesame Street as they learn about making themselves—and the world—smarter, stronger, and kinder.

—Sincerely, the Editors at Sesame Street

# TABLE OF CONTENTS

## What Is Mindfulness?　　4

## Being Mindful　　6

Be a Buddy!　　21
Glossary　　22
Read More　　23
Index　　23

# What Is Mindfulness?

Mindfulness is paying attention to your body, thoughts, and feelings.

"I count things around me to slow down."

It's when you slow down and notice the world around you.

# Being Mindful

Mindfulness helps us focus.

When I'm mindful, I feel peaceful.

It helps us feel calm and relaxed.

When we're mindful, we notice our thoughts.

"I notice how my body feels—from the top of my head down to my toes!"

We pay close attention to our bodies and notice how they feel.

Focusing on our senses can help us be mindful.

What do you see, smell, hear, taste, and feel around you?

We can explore the world through touch, taste, smell, sight, and sounds.

Sometimes we feel sad, like when our favorite toy breaks or things don't go our way.

Taking deep breaths helps us feel calm. Let's try belly breathing together.

With your hands on your belly, take a deep breath in through your nose.

# Then let it out slowly through your mouth.

How does belly breathing make you feel?

Mindfulness helps us notice when we feel good too.

**What is something that makes you feel good?**

You might feel good during story time or when you're playing with your friends.

"Counting to 10 is my favorite way of being mindful!"

Being mindful helps us slow down and notice our feelings. It helps us feel calm and focused.

## BE A BUDDY!

Teach a friend how to belly breathe. Tell them to breathe in through their nose like they are smelling a flower. Then tell them to breathe out through their mouth like they are blowing bubbles. That's a belly breath!

# Glossary

**calm:** quiet and happy

**focus:** to think about

**mindfulness:** slowing down and focusing on what you're doing

**notice:** to pay attention to

## Read More

Kenney, Karen Latchana. *Calm Monsters, Kind Monsters: A Sesame Street Guide to Mindfulness*. Minneapolis: Lerner Publications, 2021.

Olson, Elsie. *Be Well! A Hero's Guide to a Healthy Mind and Body*. Minneapolis: Super Sandcastle, 2020.

Peters, Katie. *Being Mindful*. Minneapolis: Lerner Publications, 2022.

## Index

breathing, 14
feelings, 4, 20
notice, 5, 8–9, 18, 20
senses, 10

## Photo Acknowledgments

Image credits: franckreporter/E+/Getty Images, p. 4; petrograd99/iStock/Getty Images, p. 5; filadendron/E+/Getty Images, p. 6; JGI/Daniel Grill/Tetra images/Getty Images, p. 7; mgstudyo/E+/Getty Images, p. 8; Mayur Kakade/Moment/Getty Images, p. 9; JohnAlexandr/iStock/Getty Images, p. 10; StockPlanets/E+/Getty Images, p. 11; Christian Adams/The Image Bank/Getty Images, p. 12; szefei/iStock/Getty Images, p. 13; FatCamera/E+/Getty Images, p. 14; Tang Ming Tung/Stone/Getty Images, p. 15; Tomwang112/iStock/Getty Images, p. 16; knape/E+/Getty Images, p. 17; Ariel Skelley/DigitalVision/Getty Images, p. 18; WHL/Tetra images/Getty Images, p. 19; monkeybusinessimages/iStock/Getty Images, p. 20.

Copyright © 2024 Sesame Workshop®, Sesame Street®, and associated characters, trademarks, and design elements are owned and licensed by Sesame Workshop. All rights reserved.

International copyright secured. No part of this book may be reproduced, stored in a retrieval system, or transmitted in any form or by any means—electronic, mechanical, photocopying, recording, or otherwise—without the prior written permission of Lerner Publishing Group, Inc., except for the inclusion of brief quotations in an acknowledged review.

Lerner Publications Company
An imprint of Lerner Publishing Group, Inc.
241 First Avenue North
Minneapolis, MN 55401 USA

For reading levels and more information, look up this title at www.lernerbooks.com.

Main body text set in Billy Infant. Typeface provided by SparkyType.

**Photo Editor:** Annie Zheng **Designer:** Emily Harris
**Lerner team:** Connie Kuhnz

### Library of Congress Cataloging-in-Publication Data

Names: Lewis, Katherine, 1996- author.
Title: Counting breaths with the count : a book about mindfulness / Katherine Lewis.
Description: Minneapolis : Lerner Publications, [2024] | Series: Sesame Street character guides | Includes bibliographical references and index. | Audience: Ages 4-8 | Audience: Grades K-1 | Summary: "Discover how to slow down and take a deep breath with friends from Sesame Street. Young readers learn what mindfulness is, how they can use it in their everyday lives, and much more"— Provided by publisher.
Identifiers: LCCN 2022038369 (print) | LCCN 2022038370 (ebook) | ISBN 9781728486802 (library binding) | ISBN 9798765603864 (paperback) | ISBN 9798765600870 (ebook)
Subjects: LCSH: Mindfulness (Psychology)—Juvenile literature. | Breathing exercises—Juvenile literature.
Classification: LCC BF637.M56 L49 2024 (print) | LCC BF637.M56 (ebook) | DDC 158.1/3—dc23/eng20230119

LC record available at https://lccn.loc.gov/2022038369
LC ebook record available at https://lccn.loc.gov/2022038370

Manufactured in the United States of America
1-52693-50864-2/16/2023